T0153329

THE LITTLE BOOK OF
SHERLOCK
HOLMES

Published by OH!
20 Mortimer Street
London W1T 3JW

Text © 2020 OH!
Design © 2020 OH!

ISBN 978-1-91161-064-9

Editorial: Laura Doulton
Project manager: Russell Porter
Design: Tony Seddon
Production: Rachel Burgess

A CIP catalogue record for this book is available from the British Library

Printed in Dubai

10 9 8 7 6 5 4 3 2 1

Cover image: OSTILL/Franck Camhi/Shutterstock

THE LITTLE BOOK OF
SHERLOCK HOLMES

ELEMENTARY WIT & WISDOM

with original illustrations by
SIDNEY PAGET

CONTENTS

INTRODUCTION – 6

8
....
CHAPTER
ONE
....
MY NAME IS
SHERLOCK
HOLMES

52
....
CHAPTER
TWO
....
ELEMENTARY

74
....
CHAPTER
THREE
....
FRIENDS
AND FOES

128

C H A P T E R
FIVE

DEDUCTION AND
REASONING

110

C H A P T E R
FOUR

THE GAME
IS AFOOT

150

C H A P T E R
SIX

WISDOM
AND WIT

INTRODUCTION

Since his creation in 1887, Sherlock Holmes, the world's most famous fictional detective, is arguably one of the best-loved literary characters of all time.

The Sherlock Holmes adventures – eventually totalling four novels and 58 short stories – were written by Scottish author Sir Arthur Conan Doyle between 1887 and 1927. Over a century later – and despite Doyle's attempts to kill off his detective in 1893 – the larger-than-life character has appeared in numerous stage adaptions, graced the pages of comic books, and, according to the *Guinness World Records*, is the world's most portrayed literary character in film and television history.

Best known for his extraordinary skills of deduction and reasoning, Holmes is no ordinary sleuth. Clearly a man ahead of his time, he believes that the art of detection is an exact science and should be treated in a cold, detached manner. In Doyle's debut novel, *A Study in Scarlet* (1887), Holmes' loyal sidekick, Dr Watson, exclaims, "I had no idea such individuals did exist outside of stories."

In Holmes, we discover a crime-solving genius, a sharp-tongued eccentric and an often-conceited man who abhors "the dull routine of existence". Dr Watson describes his friend as "the most perfect reasoning and observing machine that the world has seen".

Holmes often chides Dr Watson for allowing his heart to rule his head and is quickly impatient with those who fail to discern the obvious facts in a case. But through Doyle's beautifully written dialogue, it is impossible not to warm to Holmes. His flaws (he openly admits to having many), his humour and wisdom, his softer side when it is occasionally glimpsed, and his obvious affection for Dr Watson all make for a thoroughly beguiling character.

The quotes in this Little Book capture the essence of Sherlock Holmes: his haughty declarations, his pearls of wisdom, his witty exclamations, and his intriguing interactions with friends and foes. So, without further ado, come, reader, come at once – for "the game is afoot!"

CHAPTER
ONE

MY NAME
IS SHERLOCK
HOLMES

In his own words, Sherlock
Holmes is "the world's only
consulting detective... the
first and the last".
Aloof, arrogant and eccentric
– but for all that, strangely
likeable – his character is
endlessly intriguing.

"**M**y name is Sherlock Holmes.
It is my business to know what
other people do not know."

Holmes,
"The Adventure of the Blue Carbuncle",
The Strand Magazine, 1892

"The only unofficial consulting detective," he answered. "I am the last and highest court of appeal in detection."

Holmes,
The Sign of The Four, 1890

"I am a brain, Watson. The rest of me is a mere appendix."

Holmes,
"The Adventure of the Mazarin Stone",
The Strand Magazine, 1921

Arthur Conan Doyle
originally named his famous
detective "Sherrinford".

The author's love of cricket led
him to "Sherlock" – it was
said to be a combination of the
names of two Nottinghamshire
cricketers he admired,
Sherwin and Shacklock.

"I abhor the dull routine of existence. I crave for mental exaltation. That is why I have chosen my own particular profession, or rather created it, for I am the only one in the world."

Holmes,
The Sign of The Four, 1890

Holmes was working hard over a chemical investigation.
Illustration from "The Adventure of the Naval Treaty", 1893

"You are Holmes, the meddler."

My friend smiled.

"Holmes, the busybody!"

His smile broadened.

"Holmes, the Scotland Yard Jack-in-office!"

Holmes chuckled heartily.

Dr Watson recounts Holmes' meeting
with Dr Grimesby Roylott, "The Adventure of the
Speckled Band", *The Strand Magazine*, 1892

"This fellow may be very clever," I said to myself, "but he is certainly very conceited."

Dr Watson on Holmes,
A Study in Scarlet, 1887

"You remind me of Edgar Allan Poe's Dupin. I had no idea that such individuals did exist outside of stories."

Dr Watson to Holmes,
A Study in Scarlet, 1887

"My mind… rebels at stagnation. Give me problems, give me work, give me the most abstruse cryptogram or the most intricate analysis, and I am in my own proper atmosphere. I can dispense then with artificial stimulants."

Holmes,
The Sign of the Four, 1890

"And now, Doctor, we've done our work, so it's time we had some play. A sandwich and a cup of coffee, and then off to violin-land, where all is sweetness and delicacy and harmony, and there are no red-headed clients to vex us with their conundrums."

Holmes to Dr Watson,
"The Red-Headed League",
The Strand Magazine, 1891

Doyle's inspiration for
Holmes was Dr Joseph Bell,
a renowned surgeon and lecturer
at Edinburgh University.

Doyle studied under him and
admired Bell's knack for making
detailed observations before
reaching a diagnosis.

"There is nothing more to be said or to be done tonight, so hand me over my violin and let us try to forget for half an hour the miserable weather and the still more miserable ways of our fellowmen."

Holmes,
"The Five Orange Pips",
The Strand Magazine, 1891

"Let me see – what are my other shortcomings? I get in the dumps at times, and don't open my mouth for days on end. You must not think I am sulky when I do that. Just let me alone, and I'll soon be right."

Holmes, *A Study in Scarlet*, 1887

But now and again a reaction would seize him, and for days on end he would lie upon the sofa in the sitting-room, hardly uttering a word or moving a muscle from morning to night...

… On these occasions I have noticed such a dreamy, vacant expression in his eyes, that I might have suspected him of being addicted to the use of some narcotic, had not the temperance and cleanliness of his whole life forbidden such a notion.

Dr Watson on Holmes,
A Study in Scarlet, 1887

A curious collection.
Illustration from "The Musgrave Ritual", 1893

"You know a conjurer gets no credit when once he has explained his trick; and if I show you too much of my method of working, you will come to the conclusion that I am a very ordinary individual after all."

Holmes,
A Study in Scarlet, 1887

1. Knowledge of Literature: *Nil.*

2. Knowledge of Philosophy: *Nil.*

3. Knowledge of Astronomy: *Nil.*

4. Knowledge of Politics: *Feeble.*

5. Knowledge of Botany: *Variable.*
   Well up in belladonna, opium, and poisons generally. Knows nothing of practical gardening.

6. Knowledge of Geology: *Practical, but limited. Tells at a glance different soils from each other. After walks has shown me splashes upon his trousers, and told me by their colour and consistence in what part of London he had received them.*

7. Knowledge of Chemistry: *Profound.*

8. Knowledge of Anatomy: *Accurate, but unsystematic.*

continued overleaf

9. Knowledge of Sensational Literature: *Immense. He appears to know every detail of every horror perpetrated in the century.*

10. Plays the violin well.

11. Is an expert singlestick player, boxer and swordsman.

12. Has a good practical knowledge of British law.

Dr Watson summarises
Holmes' capabilities and limits,
A Study in Scarlet, 1887

Doyle wrote 60
Sherlock Holmes adventures
in total – 56 short stories
and four full-length novels.

He said his favourite story was
"The Adventure of the
Speckled Band", published
in 1892.

His ignorance was as remarkable as his knowledge… My surprise reached a climax, however, when I found incidentally that he was ignorant of… the composition of the Solar System. That any civilized human being in this nineteenth century should not be aware that

the earth travelled round the sun
appeared to be to me such an
extraordinary fact that I could
hardly realize it.

"You appear to be astonished,"
he said, smiling at my expression
of surprise. "Now that I do know
it I shall do my best to forget it."

Dr Watson on Holmes,
A Study in Scarlet, 1887

Leaning back in his arm-chair of an evening, he would close his eyes and scrape carelessly at the fiddle which was thrown across his knee. Sometimes the chords were sonorous and melancholy. Occasionally they were fantastic and cheerful…

… Clearly they reflected the thoughts which possessed him, but whether the music aided those thoughts, or whether the playing was simply the result of a whim or fancy, was more than I could determine.

Dr Watson on Holmes,
A Study in Scarlet, 1887

He was… the most perfect reasoning and observing machine that the world has seen, but as a lover he would have placed himself in a false position. He never spoke of the softer passions, save with a gibe and a sneer. They were admirable things for the observer – excellent for drawing the veil from men's motives and actions. But for the trained observer…

… to admit such intrusions into his own delicate and finely adjusted temperament was to introduce a distracting factor which might throw a doubt upon all his mental results. Grit in a sensitive instrument, or a crack in one of his own high-power lenses, would not be more disturbing than a strong emotion in a nature such as his.

Dr Watson on Holmes, "A Scandal in Bohemia",
The Strand Magazine, 1891

One of Sherlock Holmes' defects – if indeed, one may call it a defect – was that he was exceedingly loath to communicate his full plans to any other person until the instant of their fulfillment.

Dr Watson on Holmes,
The Hound of the Baskervilles,
1902

Doyle wrote his first
Sherlock Holmes story,
A Study in Scarlet (1887),
at the age of 27.

It was written in just three
weeks while he was running a
doctor's surgery in Portsmouth.
It was rejected several times
before being published in
Beeton's Christmas Annual.

"It is quite a three-pipe problem, and I beg that you won't speak to me for fifty minutes."

Holmes,
"The Red-Headed League",
The Strand Magazine, 1891

Holmes pulled out his watch.

Illustration from "The Adventure of the Greek Interpreter", 1893

It was difficult to refuse any of Sherlock Holmes' requests, for they were always so exceedingly definite, and put forward with such a quiet air of mastery.

Dr Watson,
"The Man with the Twisted Lip",
The Strand Magazine, 1891

His incredible untidiness, his addiction to music at strange hours, his occasional revolver practice within doors, his weird and often malodorous scientific experiments, and the atmosphere of violence and danger which hung around him made him the very worst tenant in London.

Dr Watson on Holmes, "The Adventure of the Dying Detective", *Collier's* magazine, 1913

"Which is it to-day," I asked, "morphine or cocaine?"

He raised his eyes languidly from the old black-letter volume which he had opened.

"It is cocaine," he said, "a seven-per-cent solution. Would you care to try it?"

Dr Watson to Holmes,
The Sign of the Four, 1890

In the late 1800s, cocaine, a new drug that was often used as a local anaesthetic or nerve tonic, was thought to be harmless. Holmes uses a "seven per cent solution" at times to unwind.

But as people began to realise it was addictive and harmful, Doyle decided Holmes should change his ways – and Watson is gradually able to help wean him off his habit.

Sherlock Holmes took his bottle from the corner of the mantel-piece and his hypodermic syringe from its neat morocco case. With his long, white, nervous fingers he adjusted the delicate needle, and rolled back his left shirt-cuff...

… For some little time his eyes rested thoughtfully upon the sinewy forearm and wrist all dotted and scarred with innumerable puncture-marks. Finally he thrust the sharp point home, pressed down the tiny piston, and sank back into the velvet-lined arm-chair with a long sigh of satisfaction.

Dr Watson describes Holmes' use of cocaine,
The Sign of the Four, 1890

For years I had gradually weaned him from that drug mania which had threatened once to check his remarkable career. Now I knew that under ordinary conditions he no longer craved for this artificial stimulus, but I was well aware that the fiend was not dead, but sleeping...

Dr Watson on Holmes' abstinence from the use of cocaine, "The Adventure of the Missing Three-Quarter", *The Strand Magazine*, 1904

To his sombre and cynical spirit all popular applause was always abhorrent, and nothing amused him more at the end of a successful case than to hand over the actual exposure to some orthodox official, and to listen with a mocking smile to the general chorus of misplaced congratulation.

Dr Watson on Holmes, "The Adventure of the Devil's Foot", *The Strand Magazine*, 1910

So silent and furtive were his movements, like those of a trained bloodhound picking out a scent, that I could not but think what a terrible criminal he would have made had he turned his energy and sagacity against the law instead of exerting them in its defence.

Dr Watson's on Holmes,
The Sign of the Four, 1890

The famous address of 221B
Baker Street didn't actually exist
when Doyle came to create a
home for Holmes and Dr Watson
in the late 1800s.

Today, you can find the
Sherlock Holmes Museum
at 221B Baker Street,
although the museum actually
sits between 237 and
241 Baker Street.

CHAPTER

TWO

ELEMENTARY!

To the constant
amazement of his loyal
companion, Dr Watson,
or the confounded
Scotland Yard detectives,
Sherlock Holmes
never fails to make
solving crime look...
elementary.

"You have been in Afghanistan, I perceive."

"How on earth did you know that?" I asked in astonishment.

"Never mind," said he, chuckling to himself.

Dr Watson on first meeting Holmes,
A Study in Scarlet, 1887

The famous line,
"Elementary, my dear Watson"
never actually appears in
Doyle's writing.

Holmes does say both
"Elementary" and
"My dear Watson" – but on
separate occasions!

—⚬—

"Well, Watson, what do you make of it?" Holmes was sitting with his back to me, and I had given him no sign of my occupation.

"How did you know what I was doing? I believe you have eyes in the back of your head."

"I have, at least, a well-polished, silver plated coffee-pot in front of me."

Holmes and Dr Watson,
The Hound of the Baskervilles, 1902

❧

"Excellent!" I cried.

"Elementary," said he.

Dr Watson and Holmes, "The Adventure of the
Crooked Man", *The Strand Magazine*, 1893

What do you make of that?
Illustration from "The Adventure of the Crooked Man", 1893

"By George!" cried the inspector. "How did you ever see that?"

"Because I looked for it."

Inspector Martin (the Norfolk Constabulary)
and Holmes, "The Adventure of the Dancing Men",
The Strand Magazine, 1903

"You know my method. It is founded upon the observation of trifles."

Holmes, "The Boscombe Valley Mystery",
The Strand Magazine, 1891

"Do you see any clue?"

"You have furnished me with seven, but of course I must test them before I can pronounce upon their value."

"You suspect someone?"

"I suspect myself."

"What!"

"Of coming to conclusions too rapidly."

Miss Harrison and Holmes, "The Adventure of the Naval Treaty", *The Strand Magazine*, 1893

Holmes is probably most famous for his extraordinary "deductive" reasoning skills. However, technically they should be named "abductive" reasoning skills since they are focused on observing a situation to create a hypothesis. By contrast, deductive reasoning is working from a set of facts to derive something specific.

He held it up.

Illustration from "The Adventure of the Yellow Face", 1893

ELEMENTARY!

"On the contrary, Watson, you can see everything. You fail, however, to reason from what you see. You are too timid in drawing your inferences."

Holmes to Dr Watson,
"The Adventure of the Blue Carbuncle",
The Strand Magazine, 1892

"**B**eyond the obvious facts
that he has at some time done
manual labour, that he takes
snuff, that he is a Freemason,
that he has been in China, and
that he has done a considerable
amount of writing lately, I can
deduce nothing else."

Holmes makes a quick assessment
of Mr Jabez Wilson,
"The Adventure of the Red Headed League",
The Strand Magazine, 1891

"How often have I said to you that when you have eliminated the impossible, whatever remains, however improbable, must be the truth?"

Holmes to Dr Watson,
The Sign of the Four, 1890

"**Y**ou see, but you do not observe.
The distinction is clear."

Holmes to Dr Watson,
"A Scandal in Bohemia", *The Strand Magazine*, 1891

"Is there any other point to which you would wish to draw my attention?"

"To the curious incident of the dog in the night-time."

"The dog did nothing in the night-time."

"That was the curious incident," remarked Sherlock Holmes.

Inspector Gregory (Scotland Yard) and Holmes,
"The Adventure of Silver Blaze", *The Strand Magazine*, 1892

I am delighted that you have come down, Mr. Holmes.

Illustration from "The Adventure of Silver Blaze", 1892

"By the way Holmes," I added, "I have no doubt the connection between my boots and a Turkish bath is a perfectly self-evident one to a logical mind, and yet I should be obliged to you if you would indicate it."

"The train of reasoning is not very obscure, Watson," said Holmes with a mischievous twinkle…

…"It belongs to the elementary class of deduction which I should illustrate if I were to ask you who shared your cab in your drive this morning."

Dr Watson and Holmes,
"The Disappearance of Lady Frances Carfax",
The Strand Magazine, 1911

Holmes gave me a sketch of the events.
Illustration from "The Adventure of Silver Blaze", 1893

"Circumstantial evidence is a very tricky thing," answered Holmes thoughtfully. "It may seem to point very straight to one thing, but if you shift your own point of view a little, you may find it pointing in an equally uncompromising manner to something entirely different."

Holmes,
"The Boscombe Valley Mystery",
The Strand Magazine, 1891

CHAPTER
THREE

FRIENDS
AND FOES

From his close partnership
with Dr Watson to his dealings
with the long-suffering
Mrs Hudson or his arch enemy,
Professor Moriarty, Holmes'
interactions with others
reveal both the man and the
detective.

"You're not hurt, Watson? For God's sake, say that you are not hurt!"

It was worth a wound; it was worth many wounds; to know the depth of loyalty and love which lay behind that cold mask. The clear, hard eyes were dimmed for a moment, and the firm lips were shaking…

… For the one and only time I caught a glimpse of a great heart as well as of a great brain. All my years of humble but single-minded service culminated in that moment of revelation.

Holmes and Dr Watson after the latter
is shot and wounded,
"The Adventure of the Three Garridebs",
The Strand Magazine, 1924

"He has the tidiest and most orderly brain, with the greatest capacity for storing facts, of any man living... All other men are specialists, but his specialism is omniscience."

Holmes on his brother, Mycroft Holmes,
"The Adventure of the Bruce-Partington Plans",
The Strand Magazine, 1908

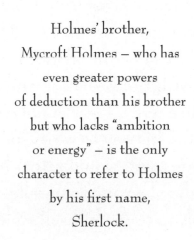

Holmes' brother,
Mycroft Holmes – who has
even greater powers
of deduction than his brother
but who lacks "ambition
or energy" – is the only
character to refer to Holmes
by his first name,
Sherlock.

"**I**f the art of the detective began and ended in reasoning from an arm-chair, my brother would be the greatest criminal agent that ever lived. But he has no ambition and no energy. He will not even go out of his way to verify his own solutions, and would rather be considered wrong than take the trouble to prove himself right."

Holmes on his brother, Mycroft Holmes,
"The Adventure of the Greek Interpreter",
The Strand Magazine, 1893

Come in, said he, blandly.
Illustration from "The Adventure of the Greek Interpreter", 1893

"He [Moriarty] is the Napoleon of crime, Watson. He is the organiser of half that is evil and nearly all that is undetected in this great city. He is a genius, a philosopher, an abstract thinker. He has a brain of the first order."

Holmes on Professor Moriarty,
"The Final Problem",
The Strand Magazine, 1893

"Sometime when you have a year or two to spare I commend to you the study of Professor Moriarty."

Professor Moriarty to Holmes,
The Valley of Fear,
1915

"You know my powers, my dear Watson, and yet at the end of three months I was forced to confess that I had at last met an antagonist who was my intellectual equal."

Holmes on Professor Moriarty,
"The Final Problem",
The Strand Magazine, 1893

"That is not danger," said [Moriarty]. "It is inevitable destruction. You stand in the way not merely of an individual, but of a mighty organisation, the full extent of which you, with all your cleverness, have been unable to realise. You must stand clear, Mr Holmes, or be trodden underfoot."

Professor Moriarty to Holmes, "The Final Problem",
The Strand Magazine, 1893

"It has been a duel between you and me, Mr Holmes… You hope to beat me. I tell you that you will never beat me. If you are clever enough to bring destruction on me, rest assured that I shall do as much to you."

Professor Moriarty to Holmes,
"The Final Problem",
The Strand Magazine, 1893

Doyle decided to
kill Holmes off by having him
fall from a cliff while battling
with Professor Moriarty in
"The Final Problem" (1893).

In a letter to a friend, the
author wrote, "I have had such
an overdose of him that I feel
towards him as I do towards
paté de foie gras, of which I once
ate too much, so that the name
of it gives me a sickly feeling
to this day."

I can never recollect having seen him in such exuberant spirits. Again and again he recurred to the fact that if he could be assured that society was freed from Professor Moriarty he would cheerfully bring his own career to a conclusion.

Watson describes Holmes'
attitude to Professor Moriarty,
"The Final Problem",
The Strand Magazine, 1893

The death of Sherlock Holmes.

Illustration from "The Final Problem", 1893

—ᴍ—

"I had little doubt that I had come to the end of my career when I perceived the somewhat sinister figure of the late Professor Moriarty standing upon the narrow pathway which led to safety… He drew no weapon, but he rushed at me… He knew that his own game was up, and was only anxious to revenge himself upon me. We tottered together upon the brink of the fall…

… I have some knowledge,
however, of baritsu… which has
more than once been very useful to
me. I slipped through his grip, and
he with a horrible scream kicked
madly for a few seconds, and clawed
the air with both his hands…
I saw him fall for a long way. Then
he struck a rock, bounded off, and
splashed into the water."

Holmes recounts the death of Professor Moriarty, "The
Adventure of the Empty House", *Collier's* magazine, 1903

"**W**hen you have one of the first brains of Europe up against you, and all the powers of darkness at his back, there are infinite possibilities."

Holmes on Professor Moriarty,
The Valley of Fear,
1915

Mrs Hudson, the landlady of Sherlock Holmes, was a long-suffering woman. Not only was her first-floor flat invaded at all hours by throngs of singular and often undesirable characters but her remarkable lodger showed an eccentricity and irregularity in his life which must have sorely tried her patience.

Dr Watson on Holmes' long-suffering housekeeper, Mrs Hudson, "The Adventures of the Dying Detective", *Collier's* magazine, 1913

"**H**er cuisine is limited but she has as good an idea of breakfast as a Scotchwoman."

Holmes on his housekeeper, Mrs Hudson,
"The Adventure of the Naval Treaty",
The Strand Magazine, 1893

The landlady stood in the deepest awe of him and never dared to interfere with him, however outrageous his proceedings might seem. She was fond of him, too, for he had a remarkable gentleness and courtesy in his dealings with women.

Dr Watson describes the relationship between
Holmes and Mrs Hudson,
"The Adventures of the Dying Detective",
Collier's magazine, 1913

"We're not jealous of you down at Scotland Yard. No, sir, we are proud of you, and if you come down tomorrow there's not a man, from the oldest inspector to the youngest constable, who wouldn't be glad to shake you by the hand."…

... "Thankyou!" said Holmes. "Thankyou!" and as he turned away it seemed to me that he was more nearly moved by the softer human emotions than I had ever seen him.

Dr Watson observes Holmes' response
to a compliment from Inspector Lestrade,
"The Adventure of the Six Napoleons",
Collier's magazine, 1904

"Good old Watson! You are the one fixed point in a changing age. There's an east wind coming all the same, such a wind as never blew on England yet. It will be cold and bitter, Watson, and a good many of us may wither before its blast. But it's God's own wind none the less, and a cleaner, better, stronger land will lie in the sunshine when the storm has cleared."

Holmes to Dr Watson, "His Last Bow",
The Strand Magazine, 1917

"Nothing could be better," said Holmes.
Illustration from "The Adventure of the Greek Interpreter", 1893

To Sherlock Holmes she is always *the* woman. I have seldom heard him mention her under any other name. In his eyes she eclipses and predominates the whole of her sex. It was not that he felt any emotion akin to love for Irene Adler....

… All emotions, and that one particularly, were abhorrent to his cold, precise but admirably balanced mind… And yet there was but one woman to him, and that woman was the late Irene Adler, of dubious and questionable memory.

Dr Watson describes
one of the few women Holmes ever admired,
"A Scandal in Bohemia",
The Strand Magazine, 1891

"Women have seldom been an attraction to me, for my brain has always governed my heart."

Holmes,
"The Adventure of the Lion's Mane",
The Strand Magazine, 1926

Doyle received just £25 for
the full rights of *A Study in
Scarlet* (1887) when it appeared in
Beeton's Christmas Annual.

Today, there are only
31 complete copies of the
magazine. In 2007, a copy
sold at Sothebys auction for
$156,000 (£127,000), making
it one of the most expensive
magazines in the world!

I fell into a brown study.

Illustration from "The Adventure of the Cardboard Box", 1893

"You have a grand gift for silence, Watson. It makes you quite invaluable as a companion."

Holmes,
"The Man with the Twisted Lip",
The Strand Magazine, 1891

After *A Study in Scarlet*,
Doyle might have been ready to
give up on his writing career were it
not for a dinner party he attended
with Oscar Wilde. The host,
Joseph Stoddart, was the editor of
American publication *Lippincott's
Monthly Magazine*, and he convinced
both Doyle and Wilde to write
novels for serialisation. Doyle later
described the dinner party as his
"golden evening".

"Now, Watson, the fair sex is your department."

Holmes,
"The Adventure of the Second Stain",
The Strand Magazine, 1904

Holmes is known for
placing logic and reasoning
above matters of the heart.

In "The Adventure of
Charles Augustus Milverton"
(1904), he disguises himself
as a plumber and starts a
relationship with a maid in
order to glean information
from her. Once he has what
he needs, he never speaks
to her again!

CHAPTER
FOUR

THE GAME
IS AFOOT

Sherlock Holmes' success
as a detective is fuelled
by his hunger for brainwork
and adventure, and his
love of the dramatic.
Always ready for the next
unsolved crime, he never
feels more alive than when a
difficult case beckons.

"There's the scarlet thread of murder running through the colourless skein of life, and our duty is to unravel it, and isolate it, and expose every inch of it."

Holmes to Dr Watson,
A Study in Scarlet, 1887

I was awakened by a tugging at my shoulder. It was Holmes. The candle in his hand shone upon his eager stooping face, and told me at a glance that something was amiss. "Come, Watson, come!" he cried. "The game is afoot. Not a word! Into your clothes and come!"

Dr Watson,
"The Adventure of the Abbey Grange",
The Strand Magazine, 1904

Nothing could exceed his energy when the working fit was upon him…

Dr Watson on Holmes,
A Study in Scarlet, 1887

"Now is the dramatic moment of fate, Watson, when you hear a step upon the stair which is walking into your life, and you know not whether for good or ill."

Holmes to Dr Watson,
The Hound of the Baskervilles,
1902

Fast asleep in his box.

Illustration from "The Adventure of the Naval Treaty", 1893

"**I** never can resist a touch
of the dramatic."

Holmes,
"The Adventure of the Naval Treaty",
The Strand Magazine, 1893

"**W**atson. Come at once
if convenient. If inconvenient,
come all the same."

Holmes,
"The Adventure of the Creeping Man",
The Strand Magazine, 1921

"There is nothing more stimulating than a case where everything goes against you."

Holmes,
The Hound of the Baskervilles,
1902

He loved to lie in the very centre of five millions of people, with his filaments stretching out and running through them, responsive to every little rumour or suspicion of unsolved crime.

Dr Watson on Holmes,
"The Adventure of the Resident Patient",
The Strand Magazine, 1893

We strolled about together.

Illustration from "The Adventure of the Resident Patient", 1893

"No: I am not tired. I have a curious constitution. I never remember feeling tired by work, though idleness exhausts me completely."

Holmes,
The Sign of the Four, 1890

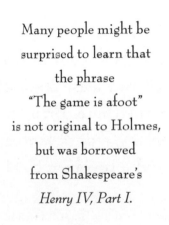

Many people might be
surprised to learn that
the phrase
"The game is afoot"
is not original to Holmes,
but was borrowed
from Shakespeare's
Henry IV, Part I.

"Am dining at Goldini's Restaurant, Gloucester Road, Kensington. Please come at once and join me there. Bring with you a jemmy, a dark lantern, a chisel, and a revolver. S. H."

Holmes to Watson in a note,
"The Adventure of the Bruce-Partington Plans",
The Strand Magazine, 1908

"I cannot live without brainwork.
What else is there to live for?**"**

Holmes,
"The Final Problem",
The Strand Magazine, 1893

"I know, my dear Watson, that you share my love of all that is bizarre and outside the conventions and humdrum routine of everyday life."

Holmes,
"The Red-Headed League",
The Strand Magazine, 1891

"I should be very much obliged if you would slip your revolver into your pocket. An Eley's No. 2 is an excellent argument with gentlemen who can twist steel pokers into knots. That and a tooth-brush are, I think, all that we need."

Holmes to Dr Watson,
"The Adventure of the Speckled Band",
The Strand Magazine, 1892

CHAPTER
FIVE

DEDUCTION
AND
REASONING

Bordering on the fantastical,
Sherlock Holmes' talent
for deductive reasoning is the
key to his success.
Relying only on the facts,
and presuming nothing, he
never fails to spot the
crucial evidence.

"Data! Data! Data!" he cried impatiently. "I can't make bricks without clay."

Holmes to Dr Watson,
"The Adventure of the Copper Beeches",
The Strand Magazine, 1892

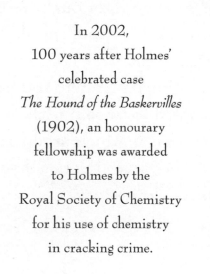

In 2002,
100 years after Holmes'
celebrated case
The Hound of the Baskervilles
(1902), an honourary
fellowship was awarded
to Holmes by the
Royal Society of Chemistry
for his use of chemistry
in cracking crime.

"Detection is, or ought to be, an exact science and should be treated in the same cold and unemotional manner. You have attempted to tinge it with romanticism, which produces much the same effect as if you worked a love-story..."

Holmes chastises Dr Watson
for romanticising an account of their previous case
(*A Study in Scarlet*),
The Sign of the Four, 1890

"**E**ach new discovery
furnishes a step which leads on
to the complete truth."

Holmes,
"The Adventure of the Engineer's Thumb",
The Strand Magazine, 1892

We found ourselves in the inner room.

Illustration from "The Adventure of the Stockbroker's Clerk", 1893

"I presume nothing."

Holmes,
The Hound of the Baskervilles,
1902

"**Y**ou know my methods.
Apply them."

Holmes to Dr Watson,
The Sign of the Four, 1890

"I had," he said, "come to an entirely erroneous conclusion, my dear Watson, how dangerous it always is to reason from insufficient data."

Holmes to Dr Watson,
"The Adventure of the Speckled Band",
The Strand Magazine, 1892

"They say that genius is an infinite capacity for taking pains," he remarked with a smile. "It's a very bad definition, but it does apply to detective work."

Holmes to Dr Watson,
A Study in Scarlet, 1887

"There is nothing more deceptive than an obvious fact."

Holmes,
"The Boscombe Valley Mystery",
The Strand Magazine, 1891

"I never guess. It is a shocking habit – destructive to the logical faculty."

Holmes,
The Sign of the Four, 1890

Doyle did not consider
Sherlock Holmes to be amongst
his most successful work.

He was more proud of
his historical novels such as
The White Company (1892),
and he was knighted in 1902
for his journalistic writing
on the Boer War.

"The more outre and grotesque an incident is the more carefully it deserves to be examined, and the very point which appears to complicate a case is, when duly considered and scientifically handled, the one which is most likely to elucidate it."

Holmes,
The Hound of the Baskervilles,
1902

"The emotional qualities are antagonistic to clear reasoning."

Holmes,
The Sign of the Four, 1890

"It is of the highest importance in the art of detection to be able to recognise, out of a number of facts, which are incidental and which vital. Otherwise your energy and attention must be dissipated instead of being concentrated."

Holmes,
"The Adventure of the Reigate Squire",
The Strand Magazine, 1893

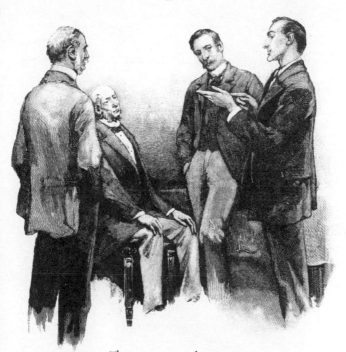

The point is a simple one.

Illustration from "The Adventure of the Reigate Squire", 1893

"One should always look for a possible alternative, and provide against it. It is the first rule of criminal investigation."

Holmes,
"The Adventure of Black Peter",
The Strand Magazine, 1904

"It is a capital mistake to theorise before one has data. Insensibly one begins to twist facts to suit theories, instead of theories to suit facts."

Holmes,
"A Scandal in Bohemia",
The Strand Magazine, 1891

"Never trust to general impressions, my boy, but concentrate yourself upon details."

Holmes to Dr Watson,
"A Case of Identity",
The Strand Magazine, 1891

The deerstalker hat
that we commonly picture
Holmes wearing was
never actually mentioned
by Doyle at all.

❧

The hat was the imagining
of the illustrator, Sidney Paget,
whose drawings were published
alongside a few of Doyle's short
stories in *The Strand Magazine*
in the late 1800s.

CHAPTER
SIX

WISDOM
AND WIT

With a tongue as sharp as
his detective mind,
Sherlock Holmes' pithy
observations, philosophical
musings and wry
deliberations are full of
humour and insight.

"The chief proof of man's real greatness lies in his perception of his own smallness."

Holmes,
The Sign of the Four, 1890

"Mediocrity knows nothing higher than itself; but talent instantly recognises genius.**"**

Holmes,
The Valley of Fear,
1915

"It's a wicked world, and when a clever man turns his brain to crime it is the worst of all."

Holmes,
"A Scandal in Bohemia",
The Strand Magazine, 1891

Aside from his boxing and fencing skills, Holmes is also skilled in the art of Bartitsu. Misspelled in Doyle's works as "baritsu", this martial art combines jujitsu, kickboxing and stickfighting.

In "The Adventure of the Empty House" (1903), the fighting style enables Holmes to triumph over Professor Moriarty at the Reichenbach Falls.

"Life is infinitely stranger than anything which the mind of man could invent. We would not dare to conceive the things which are really mere commonplaces of existence...

If we could fly out of that window hand in hand, hover over this great city, gently remove the roofs, and peep in at the queer things which are going on...

… the strange coincidences, the plannings, the cross-purposes, the wonderful chains of events, working through generations, and leading to the most outre results, it would make all fiction with its conventionalities and foreseen conclusions most stale and unprofitable."

Holmes,
"A Case of Identity",
The Strand Magazine, 1891

The key of the riddle was in my hands.

Illustration from "The Adventure of the Gloria Scott", 1893

"No man burdens his mind with small matters unless he has some very good reason for doing so."

Holmes,
A Study in Scarlet, 1887

The public outcry to Holmes'
death was unprecedented for a
fictional event.

Fans wrote outraged letters
and more than 20,000
subscribers cancelled their
subscriptions to
The Strand Magazine, which had
published the stories.

"Education never ends,
Watson. It is a series of lessons,
with the greatest for the last."

Holmes,
"The Adventure of the Red Circle",
The Strand Magazine, 1911

"There can be no question, my dear Watson, of the value of exercise before breakfast."

Holmes,
"The Adventure of Black Peter",
The Strand Magazine, 1904

"A man always finds it hard to realise that he may have finally lost a woman's love, however badly he may have treated her."

Holmes,
"The Adventure of the Musgrave Ritual",
The Strand Magazine, 1893

"**W**hat you do in this world is a matter of no consequence… The question is, what can you make people believe you have done."

Holmes,
A Study in Scarlet, 1887

"Only one important thing has happened in the last three days, and that is that nothing has happened."

Holmes,
"The Adventure of the Second Stain",
The Strand Magazine, 1904

I'll fill a vacant peg, then.

Illustration from "The Adventure of the Crooked Man", 1893

"A man should keep his little brain attic stocked with all the furniture that he is likely to use, and the rest he can put away in the lumber-room of his library, where he can get it if he wants it."

Holmes,
"The Five Orange Pips",
The Strand Magazine, 1891

Bowing to public pressure,
Doyle resurrected Holmes in
The Hound of the Baskervilles
(1902), which was set prior to
Holmes' demise.

Then in 1903, Doyle wrote "The
Adventure of the Empty House",
in which Holmes dramatically
reappears to Dr Watson
explaining that he faked his own
death to fool his enemies.

"It is of the first importance," he cried, "not to allow your judgment to be biased by personal qualities. The emotional qualities are antagonistic to clear reasoning...

… I assure you that the most winning woman I ever knew was hanged for poisoning three little children for their insurance-money, and the most repellent man of my acquaintance is a philanthropist who has spent nearly a quarter of a million upon the London poor."

Holmes,
The Sign of the Four, 1890

"To a great mind, nothing is little," remarked Holmes, sententiously.

Holmes to Dr Watson,
A Study in Scarlet, 1887

"The lowest and vilest alleys in London do not present a more dreadful record of sin than does the smiling and beautiful countryside."

Holmes,
"The Adventure of the Copper Beeches",
The Strand Magazine, 1892

"Crime is common. Logic is rare."

Holmes,
"The Adventure of the Copper Beeches",
The Strand Magazine, 1892

Holmes opened it and smelled the single cigar which it contained.

Illustration from "The Adventure of the Resident Patient", 1893

"I think that there are certain crimes which the law cannot touch, and which therefore, to some extent, justify private revenge."

Holmes on justice,
"The Adventure of Charles Augustus Milverton",
Collier's magazine, 1904

"**L**'homme c'est rien – l'oeuvre c'est tout. [The man is nothing, the work is everything.]"

Holmes quotes Gustave Flaubert,
"The Red-Headed League",
The Strand Magazine, 1891

"What object is served by this circle of misery and violence and fear? It must tend to some end, or else our universe is ruled by chance, which is unthinkable."

Holmes,
"The Adventure of the Cardboard Box",
The Strand Magazine, 1893

Dr Watson is the narrator
in almost all the stories, though
there are three exceptions.
"The Adventure of the Mazarin
Stone" (1921) is narrated in
the third person (as Dr Watson
hardly appears), while in
"The Adventure of the
Blanched Soldier" (1926) and
"The Adventure of the Lion's
Mane" (1926), Holmes himself
acts as the narrator.

"Work is the best antidote to sorrow, my dear Watson."

Holmes to Dr Watson,
"The Adventure of the Empty House",
The Strand Magazine, 1903

66 "**S**ome people's affability is more deadly than the violence of coarser souls. "

Holmes,
"The Adventure of the Illustrious Client",
Collier's magazine, 1924

"There are always some lunatics about. It would be a dull world without them."

Holmes,
"The Adventure of the Three Gables",
The Strand Magazine, 1926

"Evil indeed is the man who has not one woman to mourn him."

Holmes,
The Hound of the Baskervilles,
1902

"" **I**t has long been an axiom of mine that the little things are infinitely the most important.""

Holmes,
"A Scandal in Bohemia",
The Strand Magazine, 1891

Holmes holds his place
in the *Guinness World Records*
as the most portrayed
literary human character in
film and TV.

Since his creation in 1887,
he has been depicted
on screen over 250 times and
has been played by over
75 actors.

"There is nothing new under the sun. It has all been done before."

Holmes,
A Study in Scarlet, 1887

"Jealousy is a strange transformer of characters."

Holmes,
"The Adventure of the Noble Bachelor",
The Strand Magazine, 1892

"Any truth is better than indefinite doubt."

Holmes,
"The Adventure of the Yellow Face",
The Strand Magazine, 1893

Our visitor sprang from his chair.

Illustration from "The Adventure of the Yellow Face", 1893

"" I think that you know me well enough, Watson, to understand that I am by no means a nervous man. At the same time, it is stupidity rather than courage to refuse to recognise danger when it is close upon you. ""

Holmes,
"The Final Problem",
The Strand Magazine, 1893

> "Life is infinitely stranger than anything which the mind of man could invent."

Holmes,
"A Case of Identity",
The Strand Magazine, 1891

"It is better to learn wisdom late than never to learn it at all."

Holmes,
"The Man with the Twisted Lip",
The Strand Magazine, 1891